Here is what others are saying about thi

"Your material in *Helping Your Spouse Heal from Your Affair* is absolutely excellent. I have counseled for twenty-five years and found it well-done, balanced, and accurate."

—**Jim Velez** M.S., M.A., L.P.C., Portland, Oregon

"This is the most succinct collection of wisdom for helping the unfaithful that I have seen in my years of helping couples try to pick up the pieces of their shattered lives after affairs."

—**Lance Brown**, M.A., Minister of Care and Renewal
Chapel Hill Presbyterian Church

"I regularly provide copies of *How to Help Your Spouse Heal from Your Affair* to my clients who are facing this challenge. Unanimously they report, 'That [book] was very helpful.' I notice they continue to use it. I believe the expanded version will be even more helpful."

—**Earl D. Wilson**, Ph.D., Licensed Psychologist,
Portland, OR. Author of *Steering Clear*, and coauthor
of *Restoring·the Fallen*

"This [book] helped keep me from making destructive mistakes after my spouse found out about my affair. It also gave me the courage to be more open and honest, knowing that would help us heal faster."

—**Susan** (former client)

"Shortly after my wife and family found out about my year-long affair, Linda's book, *How to Help Your Spouse Heal from Your Affair,* came to me like a lifeline at the most confusing and shocking time of my life. I wanted nothing more than to save my marriage, and there had been very little information directed toward me to help me do my part. I found that the book, surprisingly, answered all of the questions that I had. I read it daily for weeks and followed it with full trust and blind faith.

"Some of the steps were incredibly difficult to go through, but every time they proved effective. All I can say now is that the path that the book put me on was God's path for me and the healing of my spouse. I am forever grateful for the insight that it has given me to climb out of the darkest days of my life into the greatest time of our marriage."

—**Greg** (former client)

How to Help Your Spouse Heal from Your Affair:

A compact manual for the unfaithful

Linda J. MacDonald, M.S., LMFT

H✚ HEALING COUNSEL PRESS

How to Help Your Spouse Heal from Your Affair:
A Compact Manual for the Unfaithful
Copyright © 2010 by Linda J. MacDonald

The names of former clients have been changed to protect their privacy.

ISBN 1-45-055332-X

Self-Help/Relationships

First printing, November 2010

Published by

H✛ HEALING COUNSEL PRESS
Gig Harbor, WA., U.S.A.
FAX: (253) 858-2254

http://www.lindajmacdonald.com

The above Web site can be used to order books, contact the author, and contact the publisher.

Cover and interior design by Bryan J. Hall
Cover photo by Connie Riggio Photography
Back cover photo of author by Suzanne Kirsch
Edited by Agnes Cunningham Lawless

It is unlove that makes people unwell, and it is love and love alone that can make them well again.
—Dr. Karl Menninger

Contents

Preface

Often persons who seek sexual or romantic solace outside of their marriages later regret it and want to save their original relationships.

However, choosing to repair a marriage after an affair is not for the faint of heart. It is a difficult but rewarding process. I have written this book in an attempt to provide some much needed guidelines for unfaithful spouses who wish to have another chance. My hope is that potential Rebuilders will read and reread the following pages so they can apply these suggestions where applicable to their own situations.

In my 22 years working with couples trying to heal from infidelity, I have identified certain behaviors on the part of unfaithful partners that tend to determine the success or failure of their efforts to save their marriages, post-affair.

The bad news is that most unfaithful partners underestimate the breadth and depth of the fallout after infidelity. This can lead to grave mistakes as they stumble in their attempts to repair the damage. Between 65 percent and 75 percent of straying spouses fail to save their marriages after the breach of infidelity.[1]

The good news is that restoration, while difficult, is possible for those who accept their roles as healers to their wounded spouses and follow the time-tested advice in this book.

While I personally subscribe to a Christian world view, the principles in this book will apply to persons of all faith persuasions. Therefore I have kept most of my occasional spiritual references as generic as possible out of respect for the wide range of readers who may be drawn to these pages.

I cannot promise your marriage will be restored as a result of reading this book; that is up to you and the willingness of your spouse. However, you are *more likely* to find success if you diligently apply the enclosed steps than if you rely on your own haphazard attempts to calm the stormy seas in the wake of an affair.

I hope you read each chapter like you would an auto-repair manual, with an open mind, highlighter in hand. Based on my clinical observations, I believe you will discover helpful suggestions on how to bring healing to your broken life and marriage after infidelity.

—Linda J. MacDonald, M.S., LMFT

To the Reader

Since both men and women engage in affairs and pronouns in one gender or the other may cause the reader to have difficulty relating to the text, I have made an effort to be gender neutral whenever possible, even when grammatically incorrect.

Definitions:

Faithful spouse

The spouse who did not step outside the marriage for sexual or romantic fulfillment. Also referred to as the *hurt spouse, hurt partner, faithful partner, injured spouse, wounded partner, wounded spouse, the betrayed, betrayed spouse, innocent spouse* or *offended partner*. Not to be confused with a perfect spouse.

Unfaithful spouse

The partner who sought romantic or sexual fulfillment outside of the marriage. Also referred to as the *unfaithful partner, betrayer, betraying partner, offending spouse, straying spouse, straying partner, offender* or *strayer*. Not to be confused with an unredeemable or inherently evil person.

Affair partner

The other man or other woman who was involved with you outside the marriage. Also referred to as the *affairee, affair partner, paramour, outside person, third party, other person,* or *lover.* Not to be confused with a harmless friend or victim. He or she is equally responsible for the affair that ruptured your marriage, no matter who seduced who first.

Unsuccessful rebuilder

Unfaithful partners who wish to save their marriages after an affair or extramarital involvement(s) but who do not grasp the gravity of the damage they have inflicted upon loved ones. Such persons make fatal mistakes along the way that increase the harm they've already caused and doom their chances for successful reconciliation. Not to be confused with a person who has no desire to salvage his or her marriage.

Successful Rebuilder or Rebuilders

Unfaithful spouses who are truly repentant and humbly seek to repair the damage they have caused their spouses. Also referred to more briefly as *Rebuilders.* These are formerly unfaithful partners who willingly accept their roles as healers for their wounded spouses. They do not see reconciliation as a right but a privilege that depends upon their own efforts and the good graces of the betrayed. They wisely seek counsel on how to avoid potholes that sabotage the potential for reconciliation. Not to be confused with a charming, persuasive person.

While this book is mostly geared for people who have betrayed their spouses through physical and/or romantic affairs, there are other ways people are unfaithful to their spouses, such as: viewing pornography, serial one-night stands, homosexual encounters, visiting prostitutes, voyeurism, or molesting children. Betrayers who seek recovery from such behaviors need the help of a sex addictions specialist. The added stigma, shame, or criminal nature of these offenses *complicates* the potential for marital repair, requiring insights beyond the scope of this book. Yet, I believe that those who have engaged in various forms of sexual addiction can still benefit greatly from the suggestions contained in these pages.

Introduction:

Five Options After Your Affair

From my observation, unfaithful partners have FIVE OPTIONS available to them, from the most damaging to the least:

1. Leave the marriage for the affair partner.

This is the worst option of all. If you want to create the most horror and pain to your spouse and children, this is the one to choose. Your spouse will be traumatized for years and may never recover. You will alienate your children, lose respect from nearly all your friends, and create a living hell for the ones you left behind. The icy encounters will continue for years to come, and the carnage to your children will reverberate for generations. I call this "The Mass Murder Option." Keep in mind that 90 percent of affairs fail before nuptials, and 75 percent of marriages begun as affairs fail, partly due to their guilt-filled, untrusting foundations.[2] Statistically, this means relationships that begin as affairs only have a 3 percent chance of becoming long-term marriages.

2. Leave the affair partner as well as the marriage.

This choice is wrenching for everyone involved. Carnage is still left behind, although there is slightly less torture for loved ones if they don't have to deal with "the couple from hell" (you and the affair partner). I call this one "The Murder Option." Your spouse will still suffer greatly, with losses that feel worse to them than widowhood, and you may never find "the perfect soul mate" you are hoping for. Even if you find a new person with whom to spend the rest of your life, it will not re-create the sense of family you once knew with your original spouse and children.

3. Stay but make no effort to save the marriage.

This decision leads to failure by default. When betrayers follow up their affairs with passive inaction, it sends a message to the spouse: "Not only are you not worthy of my loyalty and protection, you are not worth the ground I walk on." This approach tends to lead to a very acrimonious divorce and aftermath. It may even force your spouse to initiate the divorce, when in reality, you were the one to "kill it." I call this "The Negligent Homicide Option."

4. Make a bungled, haphazard effort to save the marriage.

This option is usually chosen by a well-intentioned partner who is clueless about the depth of the damage caused by his/her unfaithful behavior. In his or her efforts to calm the hurting partner, the betrayer often says things like, "You should be over this by now" or, "I said I was sorry!" or, "What else do you want me to do? I can't take it back." The rely-on-my-own-judgment approach usually magnifies the pain and leads to a more drawn out blood-letting of the marriage until it dies. I call this the "Detain and Torture Option."

5. Make a heart-felt, well-advised effort to save your marriage.

Obtaining expert, outside help dramatically increases your chances of saving and even improving your marriage. Such an investment brings long-term rewards despite the initial difficulty of facing and dealing with the harm you've caused your spouse. Even if your partner decides not to reconcile, you can look back knowing you made a concerted effort to undo the damage, learn valuable lessons, and reduce some of the fallout from the affair. I call this "The Character-Building and Possible-Resurrection Option."

I believe the guidelines suggested in this book can spare you some terrible mistakes along the way. While there is no guarantee that your spouse will want to or ought to give you another chance, there are ways to guarantee failure, as outlined in the first four options listed above. My goal is to offer you a road map for the fifth option that will significantly increase your chances of saving your marriage.

1

Qualities of Successful Rebuilders: "Getting it"

The most important quality that an unfaithful spouse needs in order to successfully regain their offended partner's trust, is that the betrayer "gets it."

"Getting it" means that straying spouses understand the *wrongness* of their behaviors and the *depth of the pain* they have caused their spouses. Rebuilders need to effectively renounce their old behaviors and develop a keen sense of what it must be like to be in their partners' shoes. This first chapter explores:

- typical roadblocks to "getting it"
- examples of high profile people who didn't "get it," so you can see what you want to avoid in your own life
- underlying attitudes adopted by Successful Rebuilders who manage to repair their marriages

When most of us do something wrong and hurtful to others, we are far more conscious of our own guilt, shame, and pain than of the damage we've inflicted upon those close to us. It is human nature to be over aware of our own suffering and under aware of the suffering we have caused others. Most couples who come to my office for counseling tend to see the relationship problem "blame ratio" as 90 percent the partner's fault and 10 percent their own. I tell such couples, "If each of you work on your 10 percent, your partner will experience it as you working on your 90 percent."

Betrayers often feel so much guilt and shame over being found out, they fail to grasp the magnitude of their offenses and the far-reaching impact of their actions on others. To family members, it often appears that straying persons are only sorry for being caught but not sorry for what they've done.

Common complaints I hear from betrayed spouses are: "he is clueless;" "she doesn't get it;" "he is in La-La land;" "she doesn't understand;" "he's so defensive;" "she thinks I should be over it by now. Can you believe it?" and "he only feels sorry for himself and hasn't a clue about what this has done to me."

Getting the wrongness of their behaviors.

Most betrayers only begin to comprehend the true nature of their behaviors after they are discovered by the offended. Upon exposure, unfaithful persons naturally want to run and hide or minimize their actions.

Unlike their failing counterparts, Successful Rebuilders muster the courage to identify their hurtful behaviors for what they are: severe violations of their marriages and of their partners' trust. They do not refer to their misbehaviors as mere "friendships," "harmless dalliances", or "getting a little on the side." They name these acts for what they are: unfaithfulness, adultery, infidelity, sex addiction, breaking their vows, betrayal, lying, deceitfulness, and whatever else is appropriate.

Successful Rebuilders remember that if they ever hope to obtain their hurt spouses' forgiveness (or, at least help them come to terms with the affair), they must own up to their wrongs. They need to name them for what they are and avoid excusing their extra-marital liasons. Those who minimize their faithless acts only magnify their partners' agony.

Getting the depth of the pain.

Another challenge for strayers is their lack of understanding the depth of the injuries they have inflicted on their spouses. They frequently struggle finding empathy for their offended partners for three main reasons:

- the ego boost from feeling wanted by the lover
- the unfair contrast between the affair partner and the wounded spouse
- the tendency to be emotionally self-consumed

Ego Boost.

Most persons who recently engaged in affairs had their self-esteems stroked by their lovers. In the affairee's eyes, the betrayer looks perfect. Dr. Glass calls this "the positive mirroring of the self."[3] Strayers, despite their conflicted consciences, generally feel uplifted by the sizzle of fresh love. They have pursued a baggage-free relationship and indulged in sexual or romantic fantasies without the ordinary burdens of a real life marriage. Their lovers make them feel appealing, desirable, and highly esteemed in their secret affair bubble. It is difficult for the disloyal to drum up empathy for faithful partners when the acts that hurt their spouses felt so good.

Unfair Contrast.

To add to the confusion, idealized affairees have distinct advantages over the legitimate spouse. They've interacted with the betrayer in artificial situations, with their best feet forward. Dressed nice for work. Free from crying babies and dirty laundry. Paramours' esteems have been bolstered by the spark of romantic attention, in contrast to the diminished self-worth of neglected, faithful spouses.

Innocent spouses often feel discouraged by their partners' inattention long before the affair is consciously known. And when they finally learn of the affair, their self-esteems are crushed. They feel shell-shocked, shamed, and rejected.

The blow of intimate betrayal assaults a spouse's self-worth like few other human experiences. Hurt partners are frequently traumatized to the point they can hardly think straight. They usually behave in uncharacteristic and unattractive ways, making them rather unpleasant to contend with. They may act desperate, irrational, angry, paranoid, and shaken. They sometimes cry easily or scream words you've never heard them use before.

If strayers remain detached and ambivalent, they worsen the partner's insecurities which only increases the craziness at home. When hurt spouses have difficulty regaining their composures, rather than feel compassion, short-sighted betrayers tend to view their zombied spouses with disdain.

In my observation, it takes time for the elevated view of

the lover to fade from the unfaithful person's mind. But once it does—whether the betrayer stays with his/her spouse or takes off with the affair partner—down the road, the untrustworthiness and faults of the paramour usually outrank the perceived imperfections of the original spouse; much to the offender's regret.

Self-Consumption.
A third complication that interferes with betrayers "getting" the profundity of their hurtful behaviors, is their own inner turmoil. Those who step out of their marriages are usually only thinking about themselves. They are emotionally self-consumed and act as though, "It's all about Me."

After discovery, straying spouses typically continue the habit of thinking only of themselves and their tumultuous emotions. Here are a few of their struggles:

- They are confused about what to do after being found out
- They feel bad about being caught and guilty for what they've done
- They fear facing the fallout of their behaviors, especially others' disapproval of them
- They are commonly so absorbed with efforts at damage control and feeling sorry for themselves that they lack the ability to feel sympathy for their shattered family members

Each of these factors—a stroked ego, the idealized affair partner, the unappealing disposition of betrayed spouses, and the tortured emotions of the strayer—interfere with unfaithful partners' abilities to understand and empathize with their injured spouses.

Despite these challenges, Successful Rebuilders realize their aggrieved spouses are in completely different emotional states than they are. While the betrayer's esteem has been built up, the faithful partner's sense of worth has been undermined. So, rather than gloat over feeling desired by two lovers, or wallow in self-pity over their sorry plights, Rebuilders are humbled and concerned about the calamities they've brought upon their faithful partners.

Successful Rebuilders realize that the reason for their spouses' current lackluster appeal is usually the betrayer's own fault. They know that their harmful acts—before, during, and after the affair—have demoralized their wounded partners. They accept responsibility for this and recognize that their selfish entanglements have stolen their spouses' sense of security, value, and emotional safety. Rebuilders say to themselves, "No wonder my spouse is moody, tearful, and insecure. I did this to him/her."

When Successful Rebuilders understand that their lies and betrayals are the *source of* their partners' extreme reactions, they feel less defensive and more compassionate toward their hurt spouses.

Let's look at a few public examples of those who failed to "get it."

Do you remember former President Clinton's weak apologies? His lack of contrition? His initial attempts to evade the truth through being technically correct ("I did not have sexual relations with that woman")? Did you hear his later admissions of wrongdoing and get the feeling something was missing (at that time)?

And what about presidential hopeful, John Edwards? Can you imagine the pain his wife experienced with his repeated efforts to cover up his affair and love child while asking her to support his bid for the highest office in the land? All while she battled a recurrence of her cancer? Mr. Edward's ability to convince his wife and his staff to go along with his shenanigans is a prime example of charm-gone-bad.

And did you watch the televised admissions of Governor Mark Sanford? Did you wince like I did when he made his meandering confession, clueless as to the ways his bungled words would impact his wife and children?

The missing piece in each of the above examples was the sense that they "got it"—that they grasped the seriousness of their betrayals on their families and the additional damage from the lies they said to cover them up.

The most important quality of Successful Rebuilders is their sympathetic awareness of the harm they've caused others, even more than themselves.

Successful Rebuilders are no longer fooled by their fickle feelings. They:

- seek counsel to reflect on the big picture
- identify their misdeeds and accept responsibility
- consider the disadvantages of leaving a known but imperfect spouse for a deceitful lover who colluded as their partner in crime
- recall the love they once shared with their hurt spouses
- think about the legacy they will hand their children

In contrast to the prior mentioned political figures, consider the comments of Tiger Woods, April 5, 2010, a few months after his scandalous behaviors came to light: "Unfortunately what I've done over the past years has been just terrible to my family. And the fact I won golf tournaments is, I think is irrelevant.; it's the pain, the damage that I've caused—my wife, my mom, my wife's family, my kids…And that's my responsibility. I did it. And I take full responsibility for it."[4]

His words are the signs of a strayer who has begun to "get it." It's a shame he didn't "get it" in time to save his marriage.

On the other hand, former Chicago Police Superintendent Dick Brzeczek, is one public figure who "got it" and managed to save his marriage, "The shame of my actions rose up like bile, nearly choking me. Until that day, I never realized how deeply I had hurt all the people I loved. No one deserves the kind of misery I had put Liz through…I knew I was no longer a winner. I was a pathetic, selfish, self-serving asshole." [5]

In the aftermath of affairs, Successful Rebuilders deeply regret the pain they've cause their spouses, accept personal responsibility for their actions, and focus on their partners' sorrows. It used to be "all about Me." Now it is, "all about my injured spouse." Rebuilders do not expect their spouses to meet their needs in the initial stages of recovery. They are willing to wait for mutual effort to return to the relationship.

Wise Rebuilders wake up to how their emotions and rationalizations fooled them. They recognize that marital love is more than a feeling. It is a decision to behave lovingly toward a life partner, whether one is "in the mood" or not.

All other steps listed in this book are dependent on this attitude—one of "getting it." Otherwise, whatever actions straying spouses take will come across as self-serving, manipulative, and meaningless.

2

The Three R's of Successful Rebuilders

Successful Rebuilders face the fact that their season of betrayal will require significant time and effort to repair. Rebuilders don't allow themselves to be discouraged by this. They accept the challenge with humility. They believe that in the long run, a restored marriage is usually better than a devastating divorce—for everyone concerned. They courageously pursue their assignment to undo the damage they've caused, despite knowing that it will take far longer than they'd like. They also realize the raw intensity won't last forever. When unfaithful spouses make a concerted effort to become trustworthy persons again, they pave the way for their wounded spouses to re-trust them, one step at a time. Along with "getting it," Successful Rebuilders possess three other critical qualities; they are *resilient, realistic* and *respectful.*

Resilient.

Rebuilding a marriage after the wrecking ball of an affair is no easy task. It takes resilience to withstand all the emotional ups and downs once the truth comes to light. Not everyone has the strength, stamina or goodwill to face their wrongs and hang in there with a severely wounded spouse. Successful Rebuilders decide they are in it for the long haul.

They have the insight to know that had they chosen to run away rather than stand and fight for their marriages, they still would not escape their pasts. They realize the damage, shame, and painful reminders would hover beneath the surface forever, only to rise up at unexpected moments, even if they move on to a new marriage partner. Holidays, children's weddings, or bumping into friends from the former life would see to that.

Instead, Successful Rebuilders choose the more difficult path of resilient perseverance. They know it takes guts to face the pain they have caused and the fact that their marriages are forever altered. But rather than fear this challenge, they choose to stay and do the hard work of recovery—both of their own broken states and the condition of their marriages.

They learn to tolerate the initial roller-coaster ride of unpleasant emotions, grow in their abilities to communicate, and expand their capacities for true intimacy. They work hard to restore their integrity and make amends with those they've wounded. They are determined to stay the course of recovery, despite setbacks and times of discouragement.

Realistic.

Successful Rebuilders are also realistic. They know that the innocence of their marriage is gone. They do not assume that just because they are sorry for their offenses that their spouses will come running back into their arms, ready to forgive and reunite. They know that broken trust takes time to repair, and even then, scars will remain. While they do not expect instant healing of their relationships, they do hold out for the opportunity to earn a second chance.

Once their marriages are on more solid footings in the years to come, Successful Rebuilders are not startled when occasional reminders of their past indiscretions still crop up. Rather than resent such intrusions, they immediately seek to soothe their spouses, thankful they have fought against the forces that sought to destroy their families and won. They find satisfaction, knowing they chose the way of growth rather than the way of retreat.

Respectful.

When people engage in affairs, they rarely asked their spouses ahead of time, "Hey, I'm attracted to a colleague at work. Is it OK with you if I go to bed with him/her?" Betrayers generally made private decisions about their extra-marital involvements. Even if they fell into an affair by surprise or a moment of weakness such as an unplanned one night stand, at some point the unfaithful person made a unilateral choice to step outside the marriage.

Successful Rebuilders understand that when they crossed the line into romance with an outside person, they deprived their spouses of an important "vote" on the matter. They realize they violated their spouses' marital rights of exclusivity and privacy. To compensate for these violations, Successful Rebuilders respect the offended spouse's choices on how to proceed post-affair.

Karen Johnson, a counselor in Maui, Hawaii, says to wounded spouses, "You get to."[6] In other words, the betrayer broke all the rules without permission, so now the spouse "gets to" choose the next move. Successful Rebuilders under-stand the vow-breaking nature of their transgressions and respect their partners' rights to have choices of their own.

Sometimes the betrayal has caused so much damage (es-pecially true when multiple lies and betrayals occurred), the hurt spouse wants no contact for a while. Successful Rebuild-ers patiently respect a hurt partner's need for space. They al-low offended partners the time they need to process their confused feelings. The hurt spouse may need to see whether the straying partner is committed to real recovery, apart from offering any assurance of reconciliation.

A trial separation, in agreed upon temporary quarters, is a wonderful opportunity for the betrayer to demonstrate gen-uine contrition and a willingness to deal with his/her own hang-ups that allowed the affair to happen in the first place. It often provides the solitude necessary for the strayer to re-flect on his or her actions, undo the rationalizations used to justify the affair, and get a taste of what it would be like to live without the spouse. The more the offender seeks his/her own personal recovery without relying on the hurt spouse, the more likely the hurt spouse will trust the betrayer's sin-cerity. Down the road, the offended partner may even relent and give the betrayer another chance.

Sometimes a temporary separation also helps betrayed partners regain a measure of dignity after the shame of inti-mate betrayal. It can serve as a tangible way for hurt spouses to protest a partner's unfaithful choices and give them some space to sort their feelings and consider their options. Kick-ing the betrayer out of the house also allows faithful spouses to send a message to the betrayer, family, and a few close friends: infidelity is a severe offense to the marriage and a potential deal-breaker. It also underlines the fact that, after having no say about the offender's outside trysts, wounded spouses "get to" set the terms for any possible reconciliation. Smart Rebuilders know they need to place themselves at the mercy of their hurt partners.

Successful Rebuilders do not let a time of separation sideline them from their road to recovery or give them an excuse to live the single lifestyle again. They remain steadfast in staying away from former lovers and refrain from other forms of sexual acting out. They demonstrate their commitment to love the hurt spouse and children, despite the inconvenience of living elsewhere. Rebuilders continue to pursue spiritually healthy friends, pastors, counseling, recovery groups, honest self-reflection, spiritual renewal—apart from the security of a restored marriage.

This is not to say that a trial separation should be automatic after betrayal.

Sometimes a few days at a hotel or a friend's house is enough of a "brush-with-death" to motivate a straying spouse to be totally broken and for the betrayed to regain enough equilibrium to tolerate closer proximity to the offending partner. Other betrayed spouses prefer to have a penitent spouse remain in the home to offer hugs and reassurances of love. They may choose this option in order to soothe their rattled nerves and calm fears of rejection.

One advantage of allowing sincerely remorseful partners back into the house is that they are forced to see the damage they have caused, up close and personal. Another benefit is that couples who learn to plow through the tremendous emotional swings while living together often reach a new high water mark in their ability to work through conflict. However this is difficult to accomplish if the betrayer is not sorry or without the aid of a well-trained therapist.

In addition to counseling, for persons of faith I especially like Drs. Earl and Sandy Wilson's model of selecting a Spiritual Care Team to surround the couple as adjunct support. [7]

No matter what, Rebuilders who wish to repair their marriages respect the rights of their betrayed spouses to choose the living arrangements in the aftermath of infidelity.

Now that I have briefly covered the attitudes and character qualities of Successful Rebuilders, hopefully you are ready to dive into "The List."

The List is a set of 15 step-by-step guidelines to help you minimize the fallout and prevent further damage to your loved ones after your affair comes to light.

While these steps are a quick read, applying them is not a quick process. Although you will need to revisit some of these steps in the years to come, the first days and weeks after the revelation of an affair are the most critical. In fact, the ways you respond to your spouse in the first tumultuous hours after he/she learns of your affair may set the tone for the next few years of your relationship, as well as your life. So pay special attention to the next chapter regarding how to handle the initial revelation of your clandestine activities.

The List:

---

15 Essential Steps to Repair and Heal Your Marriage

3

Guidelines for Discovery and Disclosure

Few experiences in life are more traumatic than learning of a beloved partner's intimate betrayal. As infidelity expert, Dr. Shirley Glass states, "The private calamity of discovering that your partner has become someone you don't recognize and has lied to you as if you were an enemy blows your secure world to pieces." She goes on to observe, "In just a few seconds, the safest haven in the world is turned into the source of the greatest treachery." [8] No wonder the online message boards for betrayed spouses refer to the day of discovery or disclosure as "D-Day."

It behooves the unfaithful to handle the initial disclosure of their betrayal(s) with care. These guidelines can help you avoid worsening the already terrible blow to your spouse when he/she learns about your affair. If you brace yourself for a radical ride of crazy emotions and follow these initial guidelines, you will increase your chances of navigating the perfect storm without sinking your marriage.

1. Successful Rebuilders tell their spouses the truth about the affair, rather than waiting to be discovered.

When a betrayer *voluntarily* admits to an affair he/she increases the chances the marriage will survive. If the unfaithful person discloses an affair on his/her own, as hurt as the faithful spouse is, he/he is often able to accept the devastating news with more grace. Your decision to tell your spouse the truth up front, rather than waiting to be found out, communicates a vulnerable first step in trustworthiness, despite your utterly untrustworthy actions.

On the other hand, rebuilding is more difficult when the faithful spouse finds out about the affair through other means, such as: being told by a neighbor, finding a suspicious receipt, sleuthing, receiving a call from the affairee or the affairee's spouse, accidently coming across e-mails or texts exchanged with the lover. When spouses learn of a partner's infidelity through such indirect means, the resulting hurt and distrust are magnified. Once the initial shock wears off, the injured one is left wondering how long the betrayer would have kept up the façade. This "wondering" often becomes a source of torment. Hurt partners may exclaim, "But you never would have told me the truth if _____ hadn't told me!" or quiz, "And, just when were you planning to tell me the truth?"

2. If the affair comes to light through "discovery" vs. direct disclosure by the strayer, Successful Rebuilders show instant shame and remorse and are not defensive.

While direct admission is more desirable, the ways a betrayer responds to being found out can make all the difference. Once their behaviors are exposed, Successful Rebuilders feel ashamed and remorseful. They willingly tell the truth without their spouses needing to pry it out of them.

When faithful partners see instant sadness and remorse on

the strayer's face, they find a measure of comfort despite their tremendous pain. When betrayers choose a humble stance, spouses are also less likely to retaliate in extreme ways.

On the other hand, unsuccessful rebuilders make numerous mistakes when their spouses unexpectedly learn of an affair. They continue to lie, use spin tactics, dodge questions, or make excuses for the affair. They lash out at the faithful spouse with statements like, "You're crazy!" or, "If you weren't so _____, I never would have gotten involved with him/her!" or, "You're making a big deal out of nothing."

When the unfaithful act defensive or evasive, they invite more distrust. And if they try to manipulate their way out of hot water, like using romantic gestures to "soften up" an enraged spouse, they only make matters worse.

Later, when the dust settles and the betrayer sheepishly wants to save the marriage, those initial, self-protective reactions tend to make repair efforts less believable.

Two other factors that complicate future healing after disclosure: *prior tactics* and *threats of divorce*

The *array of tactics* the betrayer used to protect him/herself prior to disclosure can interfere with the hope of reconciling. For example, if the faithful partner suspected something was amiss, asked a few questions, only to be met with flat denials, further damage was done. The more denials and lies the faithful spouse heard prior to learning the awful truth, the more difficult it is to win his or her trust back once the affair is out in the open.

Another problem that interferes with recovery is if the betrayer combined the initial disclosure about the affair with the *threat of divorce*. Such double betrayals—the affair and the plan to divorce—are so catastrophic, many spouses cannot recover from the shock in order to trust again. Down the road, if the betrayer has a change of heart and wants to eat his/her words and save the marriage, the chances for repair are significantly reduced.

These points illustrate the fact that the ways you handle the initial disclosure can greatly enhance or hinder the potential for future healing in the marriage.

3. Once the affair has been disclosed, Successful Rebuilders willingly break off all contact with the affair partner, including phone calls, texting, e-mails, and physical presence.

Successful Rebuilders recognize the danger and damage of continued contact with the affair partner. They seek to quickly put as much space between themselves and the former lover. They accept the fact that once a married person crosses the line from colleague or friend into romance with an outside person, the betrayer loses all rights to relate to the "friend" or "colleague" if he/she wants to save the marriage. Successful Rebuilders are willing to suffer the accompanying losses because they decide to value their marriages more than their "rights" to maintain contact with the other person — no matter what.

If the affair was with a coworker, 95 percent of the time this requires a job change by one of the affair partners. The other 5 percent of the time, the betrayer might get by with being transferred to a new department where physical proximity with the affair partner is unlikely. However, the faithful spouse gets to have the *biggest vote* on any job changes. No trying to be "just friends." No regular interaction at work. No continuing to professionally supervise or be supervised by the other person.

Besides it being next to impossible for you to return to mere platonic relating, your continued exposure to a former lover will keep your partner on emotional pins-and-needles. Each encounter at work *re-assaults* the injured spouse and rips the scab off wounds that have barely begun to heal. For hurt spouses, the past is difficult enough to recover from without adding the daily threat of old sparks re-igniting or being compared to a former flame.

If there are further complications, such as children who are friends with the lover's children, or if the affair partner is a relative, the cutoff with the lover must still be enforced, even if others are deprived of relationships as a result. It is essential that all overlapping opportunities for information flow be walled off to the highest degree possible and in ways that help the hurt spouse feel protected.

Such decisions are costly. However, the initial pain and inconvenience should not be determining factors. A divorce would be far more costly financially, emotionally, and relationally in the long run. The ones who initiated the heartbreak of unfaithfulness must make an effort to accept these losses as consequences of their behaviors.

These necessary sacrifices in the early stages of recovery will increase a spouse's sense of emotional safety and result in a closer family unit down the road.

4. Successful Rebuilders allow their faithful spouses to determine if, how, and when any final "closure" is conducted with the lover.

If the unfaithful partner feels the need for closure with the affair partner, Smart Rebuilders first seek permission from their spouses. No secret "goodbyes" allowed. In some situations, a clean break along with changing phone numbers and e-mail addresses will suffice. Other times it is helpful for the faithful spouse to witness, review, or listen in on a final communication with the lover. Effective closures usually include:

- **a declaration of love for the spouse**
- **an admission that the relationship was wrong**
- **a firm insistence that the relationship is over**
- **a request for the affair partner to make no further contact with the betrayer or other family members**

If the wounded partner feels as though he/she has to twist your arm to sever all contacts with the other person, you lose credibility that the affair is over. It is best if you come up with what to say and have your spouse review it. However, if the faithful partner composes the script or has to do the confronting, your personal "buy in" will be doubted later on and the subject of many arguments to come. You will come across more believable if you do the work of confronting and closing the door to the lover, with the faithful partner's full knowledge and approval. But what if you are afraid to cut all ties with the lover? The next chapter explores this dilemma.

4

Stumbling Blocks to Severing Ties with the Affair Partner

Sometimes a straying spouse is afraid to completely break things off with the affair partner. Here are a few common concerns:

The strayer may be unsure as to whether the spouse will accept him/her back.

Gingerly holding onto the affair partner for a little security will *guarantee* your failure to restore the marriage. Even if the faithful spouse doesn't consciously know that you've maintained some manner of connection with the other person, he/she will sense it intuitively and not be able to trust you. Continued secret contacts with the lover will put an invisible wedge in the marriage, keep your heart in knots, and strain the faithful spouse's nerves. You will feel better in the long run if you take the leap of faith to completely let go of the outside person and give your marriage a fighting chance.

The betrayer may be unsure the spouse will ever meet his or her needs.

No matter the condition of the marriage before the affair, the betrayer had a lot of options besides an outside romance, such as: directly expressing unmet needs, dragging the partner in for extended counseling, insisting he or she join you on a Marriage Encounter or Retrouvaille Weekend, a bold letter to the spouse, a well-planned intervention of some kind, or even therapeutic, controlled separation (under the guidance of a counselor or pastor). Even divorcing an abusive or cruel partner is more merciful than seeking solace in the arms of a lover during the marriage.

Successful Rebuilders accept full responsibility for the decision to betray the marriage partner. They carefully examine their unhealed inner conflicts, many of which likely predated the marriage (such as parental divorce, a father's neglect, bitterness over a life tragedy, or unresolved childhood wounds). Rebuilders also identify and explore any attitudes, such as personal entitlement or self-centeredness, that may have fueled the affair. While current stressors can also make someone vulnerable to an affair, Rebuilders know the roots of disloyalty usually go deeper than that.

The betrayer needs to accept the fact that no human being will ever be able to completely meet his or her needs. In most cases, the betrayer's perception of his/her "needs" have been artificially magnified by the affair. As therapists and researchers have discovered, the hormones activated in the brain during a forbidden affair mimic the effect of morphine, lighting up the pleasure-centers of the brain in a way not possible in a reality-based, long-term marriage.[9]

If the condition of your marriage was poor before temptation came along, it usually wasn't as bad as you think it was.

And it was certainly more salvageable than it will be post-affair.

When you view your relationship through the distorted lens of illicit love, your marriage will naturally appear rather dull. You may even rewrite the story of your marriage as having been more "miserable" than it really was in order to explain these new, exciting feelings to yourself or others. Most strayers who "bond" with their lovers, detach from their spouses and view them in more jaded ways than before.

That said, Successful Rebuilders who put in the effort to heal their partners' wounds up front, later have the chance to address formerly unresolved marital issues. Keep in mind that although your faithful partner may have played a role in your *vulnerability* to an affair, that is not the same thing as *causing* it. Your spouse did not hold a gun to your head and insist that you get involved with someone else. You chose to step out of the marriage on your own. Your job is to take responsibility for the affair, work hard to rebuild your partner's trust, and offer comfort and reassurance. Then, once your commitment to honesty has been re-established and the inital turmoil has subsided, your spouse will be more willing to address any troubling marital issues that pre-dated the affair.

The strayer may feel sorry for the affair partner and dread hurting him or her.

The betrayer needs to show more concern for the feelings of the injured spouse than for the illicit romantic partner, if he/she hopes to save the marriage. Some affairs begin with someone trying to "rescue" another from some perceived unhappy circumstance. That is still not an excuse to feel sorrier for the affair partner than your devastated spouse.

For example, consider Governor Mark Sanford's explanation for how his affair began, "This person at the time was separated, and we ended up in this incredibly serious conversation about why she ought to get back with her husband for the sake of her two boys; that not only was it part of God's law, but ultimately those two boys would be better off for it."[10]

Did you notice? Their undercover relationship deepened when they discussed their personal lives and he felt drawn to "help" this Argentine woman, in the guise of spiritual advice.

Successful Rebuilders rip their misplaced loyalties away from the affair partner and attach them like glue to the faithful spouse, adopting a new motto: the real spouse comes first.

Smart Rebuilders never defend the affair partner to the hurt spouse. Nor do they coax the faithful spouse to sympathize with the lover. "But she was hurting and in an abusive marriage." Too bad. Your lover's sorry plight is of no concern to your spouse. Defending or feeling sorry for the paramour will only further alienate your hurt partner. After all, he or she colluded with you to violate the marriage and had little conscience about hurting your spouse.

Sometimes the betraying person may want to string the lover along "just in case" the marriage doesn't work out.

Rebuilding a marriage is impossible when a third party is dangling in the wings. You need to have both feet firmly planted back into your marriage if it is to have any chance of surviving. Allow no backdoors.

5

Undoing the Damage from Your Lies and Rationalizations

As much as the affair itself has injured your spouse and broken his/her trust in you, your lies poured salt in his/her wounds. Especially when you previously met your spouse's suspicions with ridicule for questioning you.

In fact, betrayed spouses often report to me that the damage from their partners' lies and rationalizations are more difficult for them to get over than the physical betrayals. And worse, if the lies and excuses continue once the affair comes to light, most faithful partners find this intolerable and are unwilling to stay in their marriages.

Carefully read this chapter if you wish to have the opportunity to rebuild your marriage out of the rubble of shattered trust.

5. Strayers who have the most success in healing their marriages tell no more lies.

Successful Rebuilders don't evade questions when asked. They don't hide information or spend energy on damage control. They are forthcoming. Honest. Contrite. And, if they do lapse into a cover-up of some kind (usually from the fear of hurting the betrayed spouse), they confess it immediately without waiting to be "caught" or interrogated. Successful Rebuilders recognize that the painful truth is far less damaging than more lies.

If the former lover contacts the betrayer (by e-mail, texting, voice message, or "accidental run-ins"), Rebuilders do their best to avoid the entanglement and immediately tell the faithful spouse about the incident. NO MORE SECRETS. In my experience, each additional lie after the original disclosure systematically undermines the efforts to rebuild trust. Successful Rebuilders come clean and stay clean.

I always tell my clients it takes *two years from the last lie* to see light at the end of the tunnel in terms of recovery. Strayers need to know that follow-up lies and "slipups" are so damaging, they often seal the fate of the marriage in stone.

One or two lapses are pretty normal in the aftermath of an affair. But the betrayer needs to do his or her best to avoid them. Some hurt partners have enough resilience to recognize that pulling out of an affair can be a rather jagged process. Yet other faithful partners are so devastated, that one slipup can crush any chances of restoring trust and will doom the marriage.

On the other hand, when a betraying spouse *continues* to hide the truth—such as evading or flatly denying certain questions when the spouse is pretty sure "there's more" to the story—it only fosters distrust. Holding back important facts (such as start dates and end dates) in order to avoid upsetting the partner will only make matters worse. Betrayed spouses have the right to know the truth and have their intuitions validated before they can or ought to trust again.

Such hiding not only re-injures the faithful spouse's trust, it reinforces the strayer's belief that he/she can lie and get away with it. The refusal to totally come clean is harmful to the betrayer's own recovery. Strayers who reserve the right to withhold information for self-protection usually fall into secret-keeping again. Soon enough, they fool themselves into thinking they can dabble in their extra-marital activities "just a little more" without harm. And the cycle of betrayal keeps going.

Consider Successful Rebuilder, Dick Brzeczek's approach, as recorded by his wife, Liz, "No matter how intimate the question, no matter how probing, Dick held absolutely nothing back. By answering all of my questions, by not being evasive, Dick showed he truly cared about me and our marriage... If Dick had been evasive or tried to discourage my questions about his affair, it would have perpetuated my distrust and fear and totally killed whatever chance our marriage had. But he didn't." [11]

When a betrayer picks and chooses which questions he/she is willing to answer, it is a sign of arrogance; that the strayer thinks he/she knows best what is "enough" for the spouse to know. Such avoidance interferes with the process necessary for true recovery, for the betrayer, the faithful spouse, and ultimately, the marriage. Hiding begets more hiding. Lying begets more lying. As author/speaker John Bradshaw says, "We are as sick as our secrets." [12]

But what about certain salacious details? Like sexual positions or recounting one's fantasies during encounters with the affairee? I recommend that Rebuilders always share the basics, but kindly ask an inquisitive spouse if sharing such intricacies will help them or hurt them. Successful Rebuilders show concern about planting disgusting images in their partners' minds, without hiding pertinent facts from a selfish motive. Rebuilders need to answer all questions necessary for piecing together what occurred (*who, what where, when, how, and why*), without unnecessarily contaminating their spouses' imaginations with shameful details.

Sometimes in-depth confessions are best done in a therapist's office, guided by a skilled sex addictions specialist. This is especially true when compulsive sexual activities are involved, such as multiple visits with prostitutes. Certified Sex Addiction Therapists have special training to structure confessions in ways that can reduce the traumatic impact on betrayed spouses. [13]

6. Successful Rebuilders accept full responsibility for their actions.

This means no excuses or shifting blame onto the faithful spouse. Rebuilders get help (such as counseling, a recovery group, and/or mentoring) so they can overcome their rationalizations for the affair. They seek to undo all the lies they told themselves for "permission" to be unfaithful. From self-pity to their spouse's imperfections, they realize no excuse justifies intimate betrayal. Successful Rebuilders acknowledge the fact that no one "made" them get involved with someone else. They accept full responsibility for crossing the lines that led up to their affairs.

Successful Rebuilders seek professional help to explore recent stressors as well as childhood experiences that may have predisposed them to sexually act out.

Common predisposing factors may include:

- a recent death in the family
- a job demotion or promotion
- the recent birth of a child
- an overly child-centered marriage
- a lack of emotional needs met in childhood
- abandonment by a parent
- being indulged by a doting parent (cultivates a sense of entitlement)
- a parent confiding in the child as a peer or surrogate spouse
- unresolved childhood trauma or grief
- prematurely being forced to be an "adult"
- learning to compartmentalize feelings in order to cope with the pain of childhood abuse
- having a parent who justified his or her own infidelity
- negative attitudes by a parent toward members of the opposite sex
- early exposure to pornography or sexually explicit media
- being sexually molested
- being raised by a parent who is mentally ill or unstable
- parental addiction to any substance or activity

Besides examining and processing wounds from the past, Successful Rebuilders let go of the dream that some all-giving Fairy Godmother or Prince Charming is going to swoop down and meet their need to feel more "whole." Rebuilders recognize that a real or imagined lover, substance, or compulsive activity cannot fill the longings that spring from emptiness of soul. Only God can fill that hole, and even then, healing is a cooperative effort between self, God, and a band of supportive people. Spiritual growth and emotional maturity require time, self-reflection, and effort. Rebuilders seek to let go of their resentments toward parents, partners, life, or God in order to find spiritual and emotional peace.

In summary, Smart Rebuilders do not minimize the impact of their actions. They face the ways they have hurt family members and accept responsibility for inviting negative or angry responses from their spouses. They retrace their steps to better understand their choices. They recognize the selfishness of their thinking and actions. They know they broke their marriage vows and freely admit this to their spouses.

Successful Rebuilders stop fooling themselves or trying to fool others. They see *all* romantic encounters outside the marriage as acts of unfaithfulness—flirting, pornography, kissing, fondling, online sex-chat rooms, secret communications, confiding personal information about the marriage, sneaking around, and so on. They do not excuse these behaviors on the basis they were not technically intercourse. They do not parse words to minimize their offenses. Successful Rebuilders fess up to their offenses with courage and demonstrate a desire to restore their integrity and their partners' trust at any cost.

When betrayers own up to their misdeeds and show compassion toward those they have harmed, hurt spouses begin to relax and gradually lose the need to remind unfaithful partners about their hurtful actions.

Helpful statements Successful Rebuilders use:

"I was wrong."

"I deeply regret hurting you this way."

"I have sinned against you and against God."

"If I could do things over, I never would have become involved with _____"

These statements need to be accompanied by sincere feelings of remorse for the offense and its damage, not simply regret for being "caught."

Hurt spouses can't hear enough sincere, specific apologies. Successful Rebuilders accept this assignment, knowing that the faithful spouse's need for apologies related to the affair will diminish over time. This usually takes years, not weeks.

After many apologies and evidence of behavior change, the betrayer can eventually say, "I hope someday you will forgive me for _____ (a specific hurt or offense)" An example might be, "I was so wrong. Will you forgive me for running to __(the lover) for comfort instead of to you or to God?" "Will you forgive me for saying _____ to you? I feel *terrible* for saying that."

The betrayed spouse may not be able to forgive just yet. But it still helps for him or her to know the strayer desires to be forgiven, without undue pressure to do so on demand.

Other family members need heartfelt apologies too. Your parents-in-laws will eventually need you to apologize to them for betraying their trust and deeply wounding their son or daughter. However, your in-laws may not be receptive to your apologies unless your spouse is showing the beginning signs of healing. They will take their cues from their grown kid. [For insights regarding apologies to your own children, see chapter 10.]

Strayers who find themselves unable to conjure up feelings of remorse, may need to seek help from God. The temporary thrill of intimate betrayal and the accompanying rationalizations tend to cloud betrayers' judgment and harden their hearts toward God and loved ones. Deceitful pleasures also block a person's ability to feel appropriate sorrow for their offenses.

A strong dose of truth may provide just the right medicine to jolt a dazed betrayer out of the stupor of emotional deception. If you find yourself detached and without adequate remorse for what you've done, you might try reading Dr. Earl Wilson's book, *Steering Clear* [see Annotated Bibliography].

For those who value the Jewish and Christian scriptures, the first nine chapters of the Book of Proverbs can inject a new sense of reality about the nature of their unfaithful activities. Many betrayers also find help achieving genuine contrition through reading King David's prayers of regret and hope after his affair with Bathsheba, as recorded in Psalm 32 and Psalm 51.

6

How to Change Your Role from Destroyer to Healer

Unsuccessful rebuilders frequently minimize their partners' pain and are impatient with the recovery process. They are preoccupied with their own feelings and remain clueless about the devastation they've caused their families.

In my office, some betrayed spouses describe it this way, "It's as if he threw a grenade through our living room windows and blew our house to smithereens. Yet he stands outside complaining that we are crying too much, scoffs at our missing limbs, and ignores the blood all over our clothes."

If you wish to avoid such damaging mistakes, read on.

7. Successful Rebuilders are patient with the hurt partner's emotions and the time needed to recover.

After disclosure and the betrayer is "done" with the affair, the offender often experiences relief while the hurt partner is just beginning to deal with the pain. This difference in timing creates a lot of havoc. The unfaithful spouse usually doesn't want to talk about it any more. He or she wishes to erase the mistakes made and move forward. Once betrayers see the look of horror in their spouses' eyes and view their devastating behaviors in the light of day, they often feel awash in shame, sadness, and disappointment in themselves. It is normal for them to want to avoid these unpleasant feelings and find a way to fast-track through the healing process.

However, Successful Rebuilders realize that what is old news for them is still raw news for a faithful spouse. While it is natural for the betrayer to want to look forward, it is also natural for the betrayed person to be stuck in the past until healing occurs. The only way the hurt spouse can recover is if the betraying partner patiently rewinds the tape and lovingly processes the damage of the affair with the hurt spouse, over and over, one step at a time.

Rebuilders sensitively stop and listen to their spouses. They validate their partners' pain (instead of deny or minimize). They hold their partners when they cry. They respect the faithful spouse's right to have sad and angry feelings about the affair. They recognize the trauma. They do not pressure the faithful spouse to resume sex.

Rebuilders recognize the harm they have caused and accept the partner's timetable for healing—whatever it takes—rather than trying to impose their own timetables. They know that healing will only occur by facing and dealing with the partner's pain, rather than avoiding it.

Smart Rebuilders NEVER say:

"You should be over this by now!"

"Why can't you move on?"

"Oh, brother! That again?"

"Why do you keep browbeating me with this?"

"What's your problem? I said I was sorry!"

"It's over. Why can't you accept that?"

"Don't you think you're overreacting?"

"Well, you did _____ to me."

"God has forgiven me. Why can't you?"

"Why can't you just forgive and forget?"

"You're just bitter and vindictive."

"Well, you've hurt me too!"

Such phrases undermine any progress toward healing.

8. Successful Rebuilders seek to understand their partners' pain.

Most strayers have difficulty digesting the damage they have caused. They are either too elated from the flattery of their affairs, too buried with regret, or too relieved their secret life is finally over to truly understand their injured spouses' emotional reality.

Since empathy is difficult to fake, I encourage Rebuilders to give their hurt partners lots of room to vent and grieve in their presence. Witnessing a faithful partner's emotional devastation brings the betrayer out of the fog of illicit romance and into the jarring truth of what he/she has done.

Such receptivity on the part of the strayer has a double benefit of helping the spouse to heal and the betrayer to have a more profound change of heart. I observe the greatest healing for couples when the betrayer humbly submits him or herself to a process of nondefensive listening and validating the hurt partner's feelings, as long as the injured spouse feels is necessary.

Some betrayers fear that honoring the spouse's timetable for recovery means subjecting themselves to years of endless torture, but this is not true. The more you resist participating in the hurt spouse's healing process, the longer it will take.

When an unfaithful spouse acts defensive, avoids the topic, and works hard to protect him or herself, he/she ends up *prolonging* the agony and reducing the chance for repair. The more the straying spouse tries to suppress or avoid the betrayed partner's expressions of pain, the more the wound stays open, oozing like an infected sore.

On the other hand, Successful Rebuilders listen attentively to their spouses' hurts. They show immense sorrow for their partners' injuries and seek to comfort their partners' distress. They realize that patient, caring responses actually *shorten* the recovery time and are among the biggest keys for success.

9. Successful Rebuilders are more sorry for their spouse's pain than for their own guilt.

Rebuilders grieve over their partners' sorrows without allowing their own self-pity to distract them. It is good for betrayers to be remorseful about what they have done. Yet, a betrayer's regret for his/her guilt needs to not supersede a deeper regret for the faithful spouse's agony.

Healthy guilt needs to be about the awfulness of the deed,

not about how bad the betrayer feels about him/herself. Unhealthy guilt becomes all about the betrayer: "Poor me! I am such a failure!" while healthy guilt is about the damage done to the betrayed: "I am deeply sorry for the ways I've wounded you!"

When hurt spouses cry or fly off the handle over their overwhelming pain, Successful Rebuilders say things like, "I feel awful about what I have done to you," "I'm sad to see you in so much pain," "It kills me to think about what I've done to you," and "I don't blame you for feeling that way." Hurt spouses desperately need to know that their betrayers deeply regret how badly they have hurt them.

Betrayers who spend more time recriminating themselves than offering love and sympathy for their hurt spouses, take away from their partners' needs for understanding and comfort. On the other hand, Successful Rebuilders seek to put more energy into healing the pain of the betrayed than in punishing themselves for their indiscretions.

10. Successful Rebuilders grow in their abilities to show sincere empathy and offer heartfelt apologies.

It is difficult for most of us to hear about how much we have hurt a loved one. Yet, when a betrayer allows shame, defensiveness, and self-absorption to get in the way, then he or she remains unable to get into the hurt partner's shoes.

Successful Rebuilders openly care about the sorrows they have inflicted upon the faithful spouses. They don't avoid the emotional outbursts of betrayed partners. They accept their partners' rights to express their feelings. They sincerely apologize over and over again and seek to soothe their partners' emotional pain.

On the other hand, unsuccessful rebuilders stumble in their attempts to "fix" their partner's sorrows by offering weak, unhelpful apologies.

Unhelpful Apologies:

a. "I am sorry *if* I hurt you."
b. "I am sorry for *your* hurt."
c. "I am sorry for *whatever* I did."

Such statements come across too detached to satisfy injured spouses. They send an "I bear no responsibilities" message. Thus, faithful partners will feel *more* hurt, and think or say things like:

a. "What do you mean IF you hurt me? Is there any doubt about that?!"
b. "You are only sorry for MY hurt? So, you think it's mine to bear *alone*? Or, that I am making this up?"
c. "What do you mean 'whatever I did'? You mean you don't KNOW what you did?"

Rather than offer shallow apologies, Successful Rebuilders show concern for the damage they've caused in personal, engaging ways. They are truly grieved to have harmed their beloved. They know that sharing their partners' pain through the gifts of genuine remorse and heartfelt apologies lessens the burden of sorrow for the betrayed.

Helpful Apologies that Successful Rebuilders Use:

"I feel *terrible* for how badly I've hurt you."

"I don't blame you for feeling that way."

"I am so sorry for what I did to you."

"You didn't deserve that."

"I deeply regret hurting you."

"You have every right to feel that way."

"I'm sorry."

"That must feel awful."

"That must have felt terrible."

"I was so wrong."

"I will do whatever it takes to make this up to you."

"I love you and promise to *never* betray you again."

Successful Rebuilders recognize that heartless apologies prolong and even defeat the healing process while sincere apologies and believable empathy speed it up. They also realize that by choosing the path of empathy, they become more selfless, compassionate, and caring persons—just the opposite of who they were when they engaged in their affairs. This requires thoughtful reflection and practice, practice, practice.

7

Rebuilding Trust

11. Successful Rebuilders are sensitive to the extreme distrust they have caused within their partners and are willing to do whatever it takes to rebuild that trust.

When you stepped out of your marriage to meet your emotional and/or sexual urges, you violated the trust of your spouse to the depths of his/her being. Intimate betrayal ruins hurt partners' beliefs about the relationship, and strips away their feelings of security in their partners' love and commitment.

When a spouse's secret affair comes to light, faithful partners feel devastated, shamed and riddled with doubts. They wonder why they were "not enough" for the wandering spouse. They question their worth, appeal, and even their own judgment. After all, the person they trusted most has become dangerous to their emotional health.

Based on the emotional and psychological damage sustained by the wounded spouse, many experts consider infidelity a form of emotional abuse. And, when sexually transmitted diseases are involved, unfaithful conduct becomes a type of physical abuse as well.

Intimate betrayal is a severe act of un-love. As a result, betrayed spouses' prior beliefs about their partners are shaken to the core.

Common beliefs of betrayed spouses

Pre-affair Beliefs	Post-affair Beliefs
"I matter to you."	"I mean nothing to you."
"I am safe with you."	"You are dangerous to me."
"You value me."	"I am scum to you."
"You meant our wedding vows."	"Our vows meant nothing to you."
"You are honest with me."	"You are untrustworthy."
"You care about my feelings."	"You couldn't care less."
"You will protect me."	"You will harm me without conscience."
"You have goodwill toward me."	"You wish me evil."
"You consider our marriage bed exclusive – just between us."	"I am not enough for you. Our sexual relationship is not special to you."

Hurt spouses interpret their partners' affairs as value judgments against themselves. They feel undesirable, unwanted, demeaned, and disgraced in the worst ways.

In reality, most betrayers don't consciously harbor thoughts of demolishing their partners' self-esteems. They are usually so caught up with their exhilarating emotions that they actually think little about the impact of their actions upon their spouses. They are self-absorbed, cocooned in their fantasy worlds with their lovers. Along with obsessing about their affair partners, most strayers spend a lot of mental energy on efforts to cover their tracks, justify their affairs, and quash their guilt.

Once discovered, unsuccessful rebuilders try to "explain" their faithless actions to their spouses. They mistakenly believe that if their partners understood their intentions, everything would be OK. They say things like, "Well, I didn't *mean* to hurt you." This approach never works. The fact is they DID hurt the faithful spouse, whether that was foremost in their minds or not. And the very fact that the spouse was NOT on the betrayer's mind during the affair, only makes matters worse.

In light of how profoundly an affair destroys a partner's sense of emotional security, Successful Rebuilders are willing to take the time necessary to rebuild their spouses' fractured trust and bolster their partners' sense of value and worth. They understand that their season of sexual secrecy must be counterbalanced by lifelong openness, honesty, and affirmation.

In order to repair their credibility, Rebuilders choose to become completely transparent and answerable to the betrayed spouse. No secret passwords or e-mail accounts. No hidden cell-phone bills or texts. No unknown post-office boxes.

Successful Rebuilders work to create an atmosphere of openness and psychological safety for their faithful spouses. This may include allowing the betrayed spouse to install porn blockers on the computer or producing all past and current cell-phone bills.

Successful Rebuilders frequently check-in by telephone with their spouses and leave no room for unexplained late arrivals home. They don't put up walls when asked about their whereabouts. In fact, they feel bad that their spouses even had to ask, as they know they should have let their partners know their whereabouts ahead of time.

Smart Rebuilders are not offended when their spouses are suspicious or skeptical of them. They know how severely they have violated the privacy of their marriages and willingly give up their rights to privacy from their betrayed partners. In essence, they allow themselves to be open books in whatever ways their spouses deem necessary.

Successful Rebuilders readily VOLUNTEER information as to their current whereabouts and activities. They are up front about accidental or potential contacts with the other person. They recognize that wounded partners feel humiliated when they have to ask for information. Rebuilders don't leave their spouses in the dark, on edge, wondering what is going on. They are transparent and unguarded.

These new behaviors send a healing message: "You matter to me. I care about how deeply I have violated your trust. I owe it to you to compensate for my dishonesty, my disregard for your feelings, and my harm to your sense of worth. I will do whatever you need in order to regain your confidence."

Successful Rebuilders know this level of intense accountability must be sustained long enough for their betrayed spouses to regain their equilibrium. And, while a partner's trust may be eventually restored and the constant "reporting in" will relax in time, Rebuilders know they can never return to a life of secrecy or flirting with the opposite sex again.

8

Responding to Your Spouse's Triggers

When the knowledge of infidelity slams into a marriage, un-suspecting spouses feel shattered on many levels. They question their own perceptions about the world, what is real, and who they can trust. Up feels like down and down feels like up. Reminders of the affair traumatize them over and over again, much like revisiting the scene of a car accident where a loved one has died.

Intimate betrayal robs faithful spouses of many core aspects of their marriages. Their sense of safety, specialness, value, exclusivity, and trust are wiped out in a flash. Reminders of these losses reinjure betrayed spouses, over and over again. Certain objects, locations, or events associated with the affair tend to trigger feelings of intense pain, fear, dread, and/or aversion within the hurt spouse—often for many years.

12. Successful Rebuilders respect the sensitivities and "triggers" of the hurt spouse.

Successful Rebuilders realize that anything associated with the affair will be a source of pain to the wounded spouse, so they allow the partner to choose what to do about such reminders. If illicit sex or affection occurred on the marital bed, the hurt spouse may ask to burn or throw away the bedding or even get rid of the bed. Smart Rebuilders will not object.

If a hurt spouse has to work hard to convince the betrayer that certain objects or places are simply too painful to deal with, further wounding occurs. The betrayer's objections to the faithful partner's sensitivities only make the hurt spouse feel misunderstood, further diminished, and as if their feelings are not taken seriously.

Successful Rebuilders allow their wounded spouses to decide how to deal with certain possessions, activities, or places associated with the affair. They also find ways to offer restitution for the money spent on the lover in terms of gifts, lavish hotels, or expensive meals.

When a Rebuilder is willing to do whatever it takes—a move, a job change, switching athletic clubs, selling a car, compensate for money spent, or go to great lengths to create distance from the lover—the hurt spouse feels respected, cherished, and cared for.

Betrayers have robbed the spouse and the marriage of far more than they can comprehend. When a Rebuilder is willing to get rid of material possessions associated with the affair, the wounded spouse receives this as a token of goodwill. It is a *tangible way* for Rebuilders to show concern for the partner's agony and the need to heal. While nothing trumps the need for emotional support, a Smart Rebuilder is willing to sacrifice "things" in order to pursue the higher value of relational and emotional healing.

Along with decisions about places and things, Successful

Rebuilders respect their partner's choices about people associated with the affair. Many spouses feel the need to avoid or possibly confront persons who supported the affair. Offended spouses view friends or relatives who went along with the unfaithful relationship as unsafe. In fact, they are often perceived as enemies of the marriage. In order for hurt spouses to feel comfortable being around people who cooperated with the affair, they may feel the need to have heart-to-heart talks with them, like, "I was hurt and offended by your support of my spouse's affair."

Other times the hurt spouse may want the betrayer to have a "corrective talk" with friends, family, or associates who seemed to condone the affair. Similar to the final communication with the affair partner, a "corrective talk" with condoning friends, coworkers, or relatives needs to include:

- the strayer's regret
- admitting the affair was wrong
- declaring one's love for and commitment to the spouse.
- asking for a show of support for the marriage
- and making it clear that if the friend endorses infidelity or closely associates with the former lover, he or she will be considered a threat to the marriage and not welcome in the couple's lives

If such a talk would not be wise or feasible or if the friend is unreceptive, then the betrayer and the hurt spouse simply need to avoid those who overtly or covertly backed the affair.

Successful Rebuilders do not force their hurt partners to socialize with people who are not "friends of the marriage."[14] Nor should hurt spouses be left at home worried sick because the unfaithful partner is hanging out with friends of dubious reputation or values. Friends who put their stamp of approval on the affair need to be seen as dangerous to the health of the marriage. Much like a drug addict needs to let go of his drug-using friends if he wants to recover, Successful Rebuilders clear friends out of their lives who endorse affairs.

Successful Rebuilders see these sacrifices as opportunities to demonstrate the sincerity of their sorrow, suffer a degree of penance for their wrongs, and a chance to offer restitution for what was stolen from the marriage. When Rebuilders show humble respect for the betrayed partner's feelings, they make much-needed deposits of love in the offended spouse's heart. These efforts dramatically aid in healing the relationship.

One situation that severely complicates recovery is if both partners have been unfaithful at one time or another. Such couples tend to trigger each other. This is especially true when one member is trying to convince the other that his/her pain is *worse* than the other's, or that the other person's misdeeds were *more dastardly* than his/her own. Both people end up feeling deeply misunderstood and alienated.

In such cases, I try to get them to agree to two rules:

- No comparisons allowed
- One person's hurt gets processed at a time

Betrayal is betrayal. Each person has legitimate hurts. It is important that both people get the chance to be comforted and apologized to by the other betraying spouse. This means each partner taking turns to listen, soothe, and reassure the other, saving his/her own hurts for another discussion.

9

Dealing with Your Partner's Obsessions

Elie Wiesel's famous quote, *"The opposite of love is not hate, it's indifference,"* applies to big world problems as well as intimate problems in the aftermath of betrayal. Smart Rebuilders realize they must avoid indifference if they hope to save their marriages. Strayers who show apathy toward their hurting spouses send a message, "You aren't worth my effort."

On the other hand, Successful Rebuilders roll up their sleeves, seek their own recovery, and *initiate* loving behaviors with their spouses despite their partners' many tense reactions in the aftermath of affairs.

13. Successful Rebuilders pursue their spouses and are proactive about checking in on their emotional status.

Unsuccessful rebuilders avoid touchy subjects with their marital partners in hopes they just magically "get over" the affair. Uninformed offenders mistakenly believe that talking about it only makes things worse, when just the opposite is true. Talking about it brings relief to an injured spouse.

The betrayal and all its aspects are constantly on the mind of the faithful spouse. In fact, nearly all betrayed spouses become obsessive for a season. It is a daily, hourly, and in the early months, a minute-by-minute battle for the wounded spouse to think about anything else. Painful associations often re-traumatize the spouse, causing him/her to relive the shock of the affair over and over again.

Spouses' fears put them in a heightened state of alert known as "hypervigilance," with all senses wired to scan the environment for potential danger. He or she may be easily startled, visually stalk your every move, and interrogate you over calls to your cell phone. They are usually unable to drop their guard for fear another, horrifying piece of information might stab them at any moment. Informed Rebuilders know this is normal for faithful partners in recovery.

The bywords for healing hurtful triggers are ANTICIPATION and AWARENESS.

Successful Rebuilders *assume* their spouses are ceaselessly tormented by the hurts, memories, and imagined encounters between the betrayer and the lover. They don't allow a day to go by without asking, "How are you doing today?" Or, "How are you feeling?" It is comforting when a Rebuilder recognizes that the affair is *perpetually* on the mind of the betrayed.

Successful Rebuilders notice any sight, sound, smell, or word that might be painful for the wounded spouse. When a Rebuilder drives by a location knowingly visited by the betrayer and the affairee, a thoughtful Rebuilder will reach out and hold the partner's hand, ask if that bothered him/her, and offer assurances of loving care for their pain.

When a movie that involves adultery comes on television, Rebuilders ask their spouses how the scene is affecting them. They ask if they need to change to another channel.

Whatever your opinions of disgraced pastor Ted Haggard,

of New Life Church, he did several things right in the months that followed his public exposure in November of 2006. He lovingly told his wife, Gayle, "I am sad that I've destroyed something so precious...I don't want you to be afraid. I want you to trust me again." Ted often asked her, "What can I do to make you feel safe?"[15] These are the words and attitudes of a sincere Rebuilder.

Awareness on the part of the betrayer reduces the weight of the torment on the mind of the hurt spouse. Sharing the burden brings healing. The more alert and proactive the Rebuilder, the more relief for the tortured spouse and *the sooner* the obsessive thoughts will get under control and fade away.

When a Rebuilder is aware of the spouse's preoccupation with what happened and demonstrates that he or she cares about the living hell this is for the spouse, the hurt partner feels comforted. This sensitivity is especially necessary when sexual relations resume in the marriage.

Hurt spouses often struggle with flashbacks and/or visualizations of their partners' clandestine activities, particularly during intimate moments. Rebuilders patiently handle the sexual arena of their wounded marriages with extreme care. Gentle hugs and shared tears by unfaithful partners soften the sorrows within the hurt spouse and soothe the torment of intimate betrayal.

Successful Rebuilders realize that creating a sense of emotional safety is critical to the hurt partner's willingness to resume sexual relations. While it is normal for either spouse to desire passionate sex in order to re-connect, lasting re-bonding takes time. Sex therapist, Kathleen Miller, recommends that betraying partners take this sexual re-connection very slowly. "It needs to feel good to the hurt spouse. The betrayed spouse needs to be in charge and the betrayer needs to abide by it."[16]

In counseling spouses with sexual wounds, Kathleen Miller advises couples to "not rush ahead of rebuilding the communication and affection. Waiting is all part of the restoring process." If couples take things slowly, learning to use affirming words and gentle touches, they "can bring the 'charge' back to the sexual relationship."[17]

As a metaphor for setting the stage for good sex, Kathleen uses what she calls "The Frosting on the Cake Principle." When you buy a box of cake mix, you don't go home and immediately put frosting over the box. Neither do you put the box into a pre-heated oven. First, you open the box, pour the cake powder into a bowl. Then you add eggs, water, oil and blend the cake mixture together. Next, you pour the batter into a cake pan and put it in the oven to bake for a while. After the cake is fully cooked, you take it out of the oven to cool. THEN you apply the frosting. Time, communication, slow touches, and emotional safety are all needed in order to prepare the marriage for the "frosting" of sex.[18]

Another way Successful Rebuilders bring healing to their hurt spouses is for them to reassure their partners about their commitment to be faithful. They keep saying, "I love you" (without smothering) and, "I'm committed to you," even when the hurt spouse doesn't believe it. They shower the betrayed with tender words, thoughtful notes, and helpful acts—always respecting a partner's space and pace. Smart Rebuilders offer loving gestures without strings attached.

10

Making Amends with Your Children

The next step broadens the efforts that Rebuilders need to make if they want to bring healing to their families.

14. Successful Rebuilders recognize the impact and damage of parental affairs upon their children and seek to make amends.

One of the most common complaints I hear from wounded spouses is how clueless the unfaithful spouse is about their children's feelings. I am always amazed at betrayers' convoluted rationalizations regarding their children: "Oh, kids are resilient." "They'll get over it." "It's none of their business."

Children, whatever age, are very attuned to what is going on in the home, as they have a huge need to feel that their family is a secure, safe haven. Hopefully, post-affair, the children have been told only bare-bones facts about the affair or marital distress in an age-appropriate way. Yet, couples need to keep in mind that children pick up more emotional data than most parents realize.

Successful Rebuilders are cognizant of the poor model they have been to their children and the damage they have caused their families. Rebuilders acknowledge the ways they have lost their children's respect and shaken their sense of security. They reach out to their children with much remorse, admit how wrong they were, and work hard to re-establish their children's confidence that they will not abandon the family. They hug their children often. They check in with them as to how they are doing. They reassure their children about their love and commitment to the other parent. They make a concerted effort to be emotionally engaged with their kids in ways they failed to do when they were preoccupied with the affair or sexual acting out.

Successful Rebuilders also seek to make amends with their adult children. They understand that even though their kids are grown, adult children are often disillusioned by a parent's act of unfaithfulness. They may suffer shattered trust, disappointment in the straying parent, and insecurity about the institution of marriage. The fallout of parental infidelity can lead to deep, personal crises that negatively impact children's future relationships. As young adults, they may suffer a fear of intimacy ("Will a current/future partner betray me?"), diminished self-confidence ("Will I turn out like my dad?"), and reduced closeness with parents ("I can't stand listening to Mom complain or watching Dad ignore her.")

Effective Rebuilders see their moral lapses as foolish and never make excuses for their affairs. Instead, they profusely apologize to their young and/or adult children for betraying their other parent and for letting them down. They show appropriate shame and remorse, without manipulating their children to feel sorry for them. Successful Rebuilders follow up their words with faithful actions. They periodically connect one-on-one with each child to find out how they are feeling about all that has gone on, rather than maintain a code of silence.

Successful Rebuilders also realize that as bad as it is for children to witness a parent's failure, there is great value in seeing a parent do a u-turn and work hard to repair the harm they have caused. Sincere Rebuilders see this as an opportunity to model repentance, genuine apologies, and accepting appropriate blame for wrongs. They seek to demonstrate what it means to be humble, loving persons. Rebuilders realize that kids need to see that it is possible for someone to recover from a moral breakdown and embrace second chances in life.

Our personal failures can become tremendous lessons for our children and adult children when we have the courage to stick around and do the hard work of repair. But when we refuse to face the truth and run away instead, we lose our moral authority, teach our children to rationalize wrongdoing, and promote avoidance as the way to cope with life difficulties.

11

Changing Your Core Character

Strong, healthy character is not an overnight accomplishment. It the is the result of right thinking and behaving over a period of time. This next step is critical if you want your repair work to last.

15. Successful Rebuilders are committed to lifelong personal recovery and transparency.

Repentance and repairing the damage are only the beginning of undoing a mindset that supports sexual betrayal. Usually the seeds of unfaithfulness were sown during one's early life and reinforced over many years. Here is a short list of dysfunctional beliefs that Successful Rebuilders seek to rid from their lives:

Deceitfulness ("What others don't know won't hurt them." "It's okay as long as I'm not caught." "I know better than others, so I need to keep my cards close to my chest." "It may be a grey area but it's technically legal.")

Attitudes of entitlement ("I deserve to satisfy my sexual and emotional needs any way I choose." "I must fulfill myself sexually whenever I am aroused." "I deserve to indulge myself in a little guilty pleasure. It won't hurt anyone.")

Poor coping skills ("When I'm stressed, sexual release or an emotional high is my solution to help me avoid negative or uncomfortable feelings.")

Pride ("I am invulnerable to temptation and above the foibles of other people. I can get close to the flame without being burned, unlike those who are less educated or inferior to me.")

Ability to rationalize ("If it feels good, it must be OK." "It couldn't be wrong if it feels so right." "If I am feeling attracted to someone else, it means I must have married the wrong person.")

Improperly handled anger ("When my spouse/life/God makes me mad, I need a sexual or romantic encounter to feel better." "If someone hurts me, I am entitled to hurt them.")

Self-pity ("I have spent my life living for everyone else. It's my turn to take care of ME." "Life isn't fair! No one understands. I need to feel good, NOW.")

Knee-jerk defensiveness and covering up the truth ("I must hide what I do and cover my tracks in order to avoid exposure and shame." "Telling the truth will only hurt others." "I can't risk being found out. Others will reject or look down on me. That would be intolerable.")

Smart Rebuilders learn to recognize these unhealthy attitudes and work hard to challenge and conquer them. The task of learning where these beliefs came from, why they are faulty, and how to avoid their tyranny is not a quick fix. Most unfaithful partners spent many years cultivating such harmful thinking to the point they've become deeply ingrained in their minds. It takes years of disciplined retraining and spiritual growth to overcome the rationalizations that accompany affairs and to undo the power of their appeal.

Successful Rebuilders recognize the need to commit themselves to long-term recovery. Old habits die hard, and at the very least, create vulnerable soft spots in one's armor. He or she needs the support and accountability of others who've been there. No more "Lone Ranger" living.

Successful Rebuilders relish the freedom that comes from living in the light – openly admitting their temptations, weaknesses, and struggles to others. Some call this a "confessional" lifestyle—no more secrets, no more false pride, no more assuming one is above sexual or romantic temptation. This may mean finding a counselor, a same-sex or safe confidante, a small group, a sponsor, or all of the above. Rebuilders recognize the need to adopt a code of honesty with their spouses and maintain healthy support networks for the rest of their lives.

As I said before, genuine, lasting recovery is not for the faint of heart. But the benefits of pursuing personal, relational, and spiritual wholeness in your life will reverberate for generations.

Closing Thoughts

"Love cures people–both the ones who give it
and the ones who receive it."
–Karl Menninger

12

But What about My Partner's Faults?

Over the years I have helped many couples in their efforts to process and recover from the trauma of infidelity. Some have been more successful than others. Unfaithful partners who humbly follow the steps previously outlined in this book greatly enhance their chances for healing their marriages. When Rebuilders make a strong effort to repair the wounds of infidelity, healing occurs all around—within the hurt spouses, the straying partners, the children, and in the marriage.

Too often, especially in religious circles, the burden for marital restoration falls upon the wounded spouse. Churches often expect the injured partner to readily forgive and even forget without expecting the unfaithful spouse to make a mammoth effort toward emotional repair and rebuilding trust. When pastors or parishioners pressure the betrayed partner to prematurely forgive a straying spouse, the problems are only magnified. The faithful spouse feels alone and invalidated and the betrayer gets away with great harm.

Betrayers need natural and logical consequences in order to help them face their inner demons and do the self-reflection necessary for genuine, lasting change. Otherwise, the ashes of the uncleansed sin and shattered trust smolder beneath the surface only to burst into flame again in another form or at a later date.

I am not saying all faithful spouses are saints and without fault. A marriage is always comprised of two imperfect people. The couple's pre-affair dynamics may need some degree of adjustment. Although I am tough on the betrayer, I seek to help betrayed partners recognize their own flaws and mend the ways they have hurt the straying partner before the affair.

However, I do not allow these faults to be used as excuses for the betrayer's choice to have an affair. As I said before, betrayers had other, healthier options to deal with their dissatisfactions than by acting out their pain through an affair.

In my experience with Successful Couples, unfaithful partners do the bulk of the work in the initial, crisis stage of therapy. This early effort on the part of betrayers sets the stage for injured spouses to eventually explore their own bothersome attitudes and behaviors that may have contributed to any prior difficulties in the marriage.

Unsuccessful couples tend to drop out of therapy or small-group support once the initial hemorrhaging stops. On the other hand, Successful Couples keep working on their relationships long after the wounds stop oozing. They know that even after stitches are applied, healing has only begun. They must continue to cleanse, protect, and nurture their relationships for the long haul.

13

Summary

The following list summarizes the qualities of those who are most likely to be successful repairing their marriages after infidelity.

Successful Rebuilders:

- are nondefensive
- examine their motives for their affairs, without blaming their spouses
- accept their roles as healers to their wounded partners
- do not resist breaking off all contact with the affair partner
- show genuine contrition and remorse for what they have done
- make amends and apologize to loved ones
- apologize often, especially the first two years
- listen with patience and validate their spouses' pain
- allow their spouses a lot of room to express their feelings
- respect the betrayed spouse's timetable for recovering
- seek to assure spouses of their love and commitment to fidelity

- keep no secrets
- do not maintain close ties with those who condoned the affair
- are willing to be extremely accountable for their time and activities
- frequently check in with spouses as to how they are doing
- are aware of and anticipate triggers of the affair
- are willing to get rid of hurtful reminders of the affair
- don't minimize the damage the affair had on the children
- commit themselves to a long-term plan for recovery, honesty, and spiritual growth

If I had only one word to describe Successful Rebuilders, it would be: HUMILITY.

While the scriptures say that love covers a multitude of sins, I believe humility heals a multitude of wounds. Only the sincerely contrite can accept the assignments listed above.

Successful Rebuilders embrace their roles as healers. They work hard to undo the damage of the affair and make amends. They honor the time it takes for their spouses to heal. They trust that their efforts to repair their faithful spouses' hearts will in turn transform their own hearts and character for the better.

Successful Rebuilders welcome the opportunity to become more reflective, loving, responsible, and compassionate persons. As a result, they not only heal their partners' hurts, they resolve their own.

Appendix:

Annotated Bibliography

Linda's personal reviews of helpful books for the unfaithful

Christian Books:

Who Will You Become? (2007) by Linda J. MacDonald

A hard-hitting, challenging book for people in the beginning stages of an affair who've lost their ability to be objective about the danger of an outside romance. This is my attempt to shake up a hormone-crazed spouse and motivate him/her to wake up and smell the coffee before it's too late. Also, useful for hurt spouses who want to understand the roles that hormones and rationalizations played in their partners' affairs. Currently found on my Web site: http://www.lindajmacdonald.com/mini-books.html

Hedges: Loving Your Marriage Enough to Protect it (1990, 2005) by Jerry Jenkins

Helpful for preventing affairs. Offers practical guidelines for creating or rebuilding healthy boundaries around your marriage and to keep yourself from temptation. When a church elder in town shocked everyone by his affair, friends were so shaken, they designed and taught an adult Sunday school class for their church, based on the concepts in this book.

Steering Clear (2007) by Earl D. Wilson

In this book Dr. Wilson presents his program for helping those who are tempted or have succumbed, in a process of true repentance and recovery. Want to "get" what it means to avoid moral pitfalls, repent, and recover? Read this book! Perfect for the tempted or fallen.

Restoring the Fallen (1997) by Earl and Sandy Wilson, Paul and Virginia Friesen, Larry and Nancy Paulson

The personal story of how one couple saved their marriage from the ravages of intimate betrayal. Husband and wife are therapists. Terrific story. Presents a wonderful model for creating a spiritual care team to help shattered marriages recover. I wish more churches would catch the vision. Both of the Wilson's books may be ordered from: www.TuffStuffMinistries.com

Unfaithful: Rebuilding Trust after Infidelity (2005) by Gary & Mona Shriver

Realistic and personal story by a couple who weathered and survived an extramarital affair. An easy read for the "self-help-literature-avoidant" person. I have found that faithful spouses really appreciate this book and wish their partners would read it to better understand their pain.

Faithful and True (1996) by Mark R. Laaser
The author, a former pastor, addresses sexual betrayal and

sexual addiction from his personal and professional experience. A great read with practical help.

Torn Asunder: Recovering from Extramarital Affairs (1995) by Dave Carder

Terrific Christian book on the subject of repairing a marriage after infidelity. His newest versions include material on emotional affairs, too. I like his graph on the difference in recovery timetables for the betrayer and the betrayed. He includes some of Emily Brown's theories about couple-dynamics that make a marriage vulnerable to an affair. I have had a few faithful spouses find these theories offensive because they felt blamed for the affair. However, Dr. Brown's framework, which Carder summarizes, is intended to help couples and therapists identify the "message" of the affair—the relationship dynamics that made the marriage vulnerable to an affair and how to approach repairing the relationship, if possible.

Surviving an Affair (1998) by Willard F. Harley Jr., Jennifer H. Chalmers

Strength of this book is the variety of vignettes that both partners can relate to. He normalizes the jagged process of disengagement from the affair partner and rebuilding the marriage. Harley is very clear about the need to break off all contact with the affair partner and has practical guidelines for the unfaithful. I would rate it as a useful book for couples in the throes of infidelity, no matter their religious faith. He has a fabulous Web site: www.marriagebuilders.com

No Stones: Women Redeemed from Sexual Shame (2002) by Marnie C. Ferree

The only book I have found that thoroughly addresses the deeper issues for women caught in the throes of sexual addiction. An outstanding resource.

The Five Languages of Apology (2006) by Gary Chapman and Jennifer Thomas

A terrific tool for discovering the most effective, meaningful apologies for you and your spouse. If you are stuck in finding what really "works" for your partner, this may offer an overlooked key that unlocks the door to your partner's heart.

Restoring the Pleasure: Complete Step-by-Step Programs to Help Couples Overcome the Most Common Sexual Barriers (1993) by Clifford L. Penner and Joyce J. Penner

A helpful reference for couples who struggle with some form of sexual difficulty or dysfunction in their marriages. Tastefully and expertly presented.

How We Love (2008) by Milan & Kay Yerkovich

One of the best guides for identifying each person's love style (known as one's "love imprint" from early bonding experiences) and how it impacts marriages. Profoundly helpful.

Secular Books:

NOT "Just Friends": Rebuilding Trust and Recovering Your Sanity after Infidelity (2003) by Shirley Glass

This is my favorite all-around book on infidelity—especially for the hurt spouse. She has a lot of clinical experience working with couples and individuals in the aftermath of affairs. She is firm on the stance of "no secrets allowed" if trust is to be rebuilt. In her research, Dr. Glass debunks many of the myths about infidelity and includes emotional infidelity as a violation of the marital bond. She does a terrific job reducing the shame and blame of the betrayed spouse, demonstrating by her research that not everyone who chooses to be unfaithful does so because they are in unhappy marriages. I spent 20 hours in an intensive four-day workshop with her and hold her in the highest regard.

After The Affair: Healing the Pain and Rebuilding Trust When a Partner Has Been Unfaithful (1996) by Janis A. Spring

One of the most notable strengths of this book is that the author does a masterful job of explaining the pain experienced by each spouse, on both sides of the equation. I like her careful approach to rebuilding trust, her cautions about quick forgiveness, and most of her comments about our unrealistic expectations of romance. In her seminars for counseling professionals, Dr. Spring recommends having each partner read and underline what is meaningful to him/her in the book and then trade books with the other spouse.

Private Lies: Infidelity and Betrayal of Intimacy (1989) by Frank Pittman

I attended a workshop by Dr. Pittman and have enjoyed his articles and taped presentations on the topic of infidelity. Frank Pittman, a systems-trained psychiatrist, is funny and down to earth. This book is pointed and challenges many of the rationalizations that unfaithful partners use to justify their affairs. One unrepentant betrayer called it "the book from hell" (which was a good thing.) An entertaining read, compared to many self-help books.

Affairs: A Guide to Working Through the Repercussions of Infidelity (1999) by Emily M. Brown

I attended Emily Brown's two-day workshop. I recommend that clinicians read this popular book first, before they attempt to read her clinical book, *Patterns of Infidelity and their Treatment*. She describes five types of affairs: Conflict Avoidant, Intimacy Avoidant, Split-self Affairs, Sexual Addict Affairs, and Exit Affairs. Her chapter on a partner's obsessing is the best I've seen. She normalizes the excessive ruminating to a point, yet if prolonged, frames it as the faithful partner "having an affair with the affair."

The Monogamy Myth: A Personal Handbook for Dealing with Affairs, Third Edition (2003) by Peggy Vaughan

Peggy has broad experience helping individuals struggling in the aftermath of a partner's affair(s). She weaves her personal story throughout the book and makes many helpful points. Peggy stresses the importance of honesty in order to rebuild and improve the marriage. The author is sometimes misunderstood regarding her notion of committing to honesty instead of promising monogamy. Her point is that mere verbal promises without a commitment to honesty is naive and incomplete. Her Web site, www.dearpeggy.com, is one of the best online.

The Power of Apology (2002) by Beverly Engel.

This book explains the roadblocks, necessity, and skills needed for giving a meaningful apology. She explains the "three R's of apology: Regret, Responsibility, and Remedy. An outstanding resource for those seeking an in-depth understanding of what it takes to offer apologies that offended spouses can believe in.

Addicted to Adultery (1989) by Richard & Elizabeth Brzeczek, with Sharon DeVita

Terrific story about a former Chicago Police Superintendent, the devastation of his affairs, and the story of how he and his wife rebuilt their marriage and started a self-help recovery group for couples, called WESOM (We Saved Our Marriage).

End Notes

1. Lana Staheli, *"Affair-Proof" Your Marriage* (New York: Harper Collins, 1995) 10, and Bonnie Eaker Weil, *Adultery, The Forgivable Sin* (New York: Hastings House) xxi. Both authors have done their own research as well as drawn upon the research of others.

2. Lana Staheli, *"Affair-Proof" Your Marriage* (New York: Harper Collins, 1995) 10.

3. Shirley Glass, *NOT "Just Friends"* (New York: The Free Press, 2003) concept of positive mirroring is referred to on pages 45, 170, 213, 260, while her term, "the positive mirroring of the self" was used in her seminars for therapists.

4. http://video.foxnews.com/v/4137820/highlights-from-tiger-woods-presser (Accessed April 5, 2010).

5. Richard & Elizabeth Brzeczek, *Addicted to Adultery* (New York: Bantam Books, 1989) 113.

6. Private conversation with Karen Johnson, staff counselor, Hope Chapel, Maui, Hawaii (February 2000).

7. Earl & Sandy Wilson, Friesen, & Paulson, *Restoring the Fallen: A Team Approach to Caring, Confronting & Reconciling* (Illinois: Intervarsity Press, 1997) entire book.

8. Shirley Glass, *NOT "Just Friends"* (New York: The Free Press, 2003) 67, 97.

9. Pat Love, *The Truth About Love* (New York: Simon & Schuster, 2001) 29.

10. Richard & Elizabeth Brzeczek, *Addicted to Adultery* (New York: Bantam Books, 1989) 135.

11. Transcript of Mark Sanford's televised confession, www. realclearpolitics.com/.../south_carolina_governor_admits_affair_97171. html (accessed June 29, 2009).

12. Brodsky, *Open Exchange Magazine*, online archive, www.openexchange.org/archives/Classics/bradshaw.html (accessed February 22, 2009). John Bradshaw later clarified his statement by distinguishing what he calls "good secrets" (personal space & privacy for bathing, birth, marital sexuality) from "dangerous secrets" (rituals around eating disorders, abuse, betrayal).

13. For a list of Certified Sex Addiction Therapists, trained by Pat Carnes' International Institute for Trauma and Addiction Professionals, visit the organization's website: www.iitap.com

14. Shirley Glass, *NOT "Just Friends"* (New York: The Free Press, 2003) 33. Dr. Glass coined the term, "friend(s) of the marriage."

15. Gayle Haggard, *Why I Stayed* (Twin Lakes, IL: Tyndale House 2009) 244, 245.

16. Kathleen Miller, M.A., LMFT, quoting from her workshop, *What about Sex?* Sponsored by the National Coalition for the Protection of Children & Families, March 6, 2010.

17. Ibid.

18. Ibid, illustration used by presenter's permission.

About the Author

Linda J. MacDonald, MS, LMFT is a Licensed Marriage & Family Therapist with over 22 years' experience specializing in helping couples and individuals heal from infidelity. She graduated from Seattle Pacific University in 1988 with a Masters degree in Marriage and Family Therapy. She currently works in private practice at The Shepherd's Center in Gig Harbor, Washington.

Along with her love of counseling, Linda is a workshop leader, freelance writer, and author of the widely used one-act play, *Broken Heart*, with estimated audiences of over 3 million world wide. She has conducted workshops on a variety of topics, such as: Healthy Dating, Healing the Root of Bitterness, The Healing Power of Apology, Conflict Resolution, Healing Abandonment Grief, and Recovering from Intimate Betrayal.

Linda is married to Dan MacDonald, pastor of Dupont Community Presbyterian Church and a former chaplain with the Franciscan Health System. They have four adult children between them and share such activities as hiking, kayaking, camping, reading, and long walks. They also enjoy doing volunteer work with Celebrate Recovery, teaching opportunities, marriage education, and retreats.

Check out Linda's Web site for free articles and other publications. http://www.lindajmacdonald.com

Made in the USA
San Bernardino, CA
27 April 2015